# Will Abortion Make Me Happy?

## Letters and Essays on Life Issues

by John C. Wilhelmsson

i

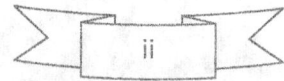

# WILL ABORTION MAKE ME HAPPY?

# LETTERS AND ESSAYS ON LIFE ISSUES

# CHAOS TO ORDER
# PUBLISHING

## CAMPBELL, CA

v

# <u>CONTENTS</u>

# CHAPTER ONE

## WILL ABORTION MAKE ME HAPPY?

This Spring I was asked to teach a course on beginning ethics entitled "Moral Issues" at San Jose State University. Having just received my master's degree in philosophy that past Spring, I was excited to so soon have the opportunity to delve into the study of ethics for I believe that a greater understanding of the field of ethics is something greatly needed in our world today. Most people tend to think of ethics as being the study of what is right or wrong. Yet the ancient Greek philosophers who pioneered the study of ethics thought of the discipline more in terms of asking the question; "How can I live the good and happy life?"

How changing the focus of the discussion on a controversial moral issue from whether a thing is right or wrong to what role that thing might play in a person being happy became a question of great curiosity for me. Yet if I was going to test out my new idea I wanted to test it out on the most divisive issue I could think of, and that issue clearly was abortion.

When the semester arrived, my class was under enrolled, and it came within about two minutes of being canceled on the very first day. So, I went all over campus putting up fliers which asked, "How Can I Live the Good and Happy Life?" to advertise the course. Slowly people began to trickle in. We just survived being canceled in the second week and yet still did not quite have the required number of students.

Then, to my surprise, the case for continuing the class was taken straight to the dean of our college and, since we had come within one student of the enrollment goal, the class was saved. After surviving all of this, I began to think of my class as "The little class that could." For I could not help but believe that the hand of divine providence was involved in the course being able to go forward.

Because of all the uncertainty over the class's survival, the first few weeks had already passed before we could begin our study in earnest. After several weeks of studying both ethical theory and the philosophy of happiness and trying to build an atmosphere of respect and trust with my students, the time to begin the direct study of moral issues grew near. I first introduced the topic of abortion in a question on a midterm exam in the form of a syllogism. The syllogism is a form of argumentation we owe to Aristotle in which several statements, called premises, are presented and a conclusion is inferred based upon their logical relationship. For example:

*Major Premise:* All things with wings can fly.

*Minor premise:* Pigs have wings.

*Conclusion:* Therefore, pigs can fly.

This kind of silly syllogism is used

to teach that even if the premises lead logically to the conclusion (which they do in this case because if everything that has wings can fly and pigs have wings then pigs can fly) an argument can still be unsound even if just one of its individual premises is false.

The syllogism on the test read:

*Major premise:* I can do whatever I want with my own body.

*Minor premise:* The fetus is a part of my body.

*Conclusion:* Therefore, I can decide if the fetus lives or dies.

Half of my students realized that,

although the premises logically lead to the conclusion in this argument, the argument is unsound because both the premise "I can do whatever I want with my own body" and the premise "The fetus is part of my body" are not true. Encouraged that so many of my students already understood the fact that ethically one cannot simply do whatever one wants with their own body and that the fetus (which means "offspring" in Latin) is not a part of a woman's body but rather something unique with its own genetic code and biological system I began making the preparations for our first full class session on the topic of abortion.

I decided to cover the topic in two class sessions. In the first session I would present all the relevant facts about the biology of a normal pregnancy, the different types of abortion, and the statistics on who gets abortions and why.

Preparing for this session turned out to be a great spiritual test for me. I knew that speaking the truth about abortion might hurt or anger some of my students, yet my struggles were even more deeply rooted than this. For when I was a teenager, before I knew the truth about abortion, a friend of mine had asked to borrow some money from me because his girlfriend was pregnant. I had a feeling that something was not right about the situation, yet I lent him the money in any case. Years later, after I had more fully learned the truth about what I had participated in, I felt great remorse. Even today after having long ago received the Sacrament of Reconciliation and having been properly counseled that because of my ignorance about abortion at that time I was not fully responsible for my actions I still feel remorse over having participated in that abortion.

So now in telling the truth about abortion I was going to have to more closely face the truth about something I had participated in all those years ago. Even more than this, I was quite likely going to cause one of my students to have to more closely face the truth about her or his own direct or indirect participation in abortion. Knowing this made it difficult to prepare for the class session both in terms of doing the necessary research and in terms of being willing to speak the truth. At times during the week, I thought; "I don't really have to do the class this way. Why not just talk about abortion as a general concept or use fancy sounding words like 'evacuate the uterus' like so many others do?" Yet something inside told me what the right thing to do was and, despite all my fears, I did in a gentle yet matter of fact sort of way tell my class all of the factual truths about abortion.

Far from causing any sort of pain or discord, the class session went incredibly smoothly. Not a word in anger was spoken, and I actually felt a greater sense of closeness to my students by the time the session was over. The next week we together analyzed the arguments for and against abortion. The students seemed to see all the faults in the arguments for abortion before I even had to bother to point them out. I am convinced that my clear presentation of the facts about Abortion in the previous week's class session played a key role in this. For once you know the truth about what abortion involves you realize that no argument for it can be a sound one.

During a break in the class I was talking with a student about a paper assignment. She asked me if she could author a paper entitled, "Will Abortion Make Me Happy?" At that moment I realized that my experiment in how to teach ethics had been a success! And that by getting away from divisive debates about right or wrong and, instead, asking the classical philosophical question about happiness perspectives had been changed and my students had grown in wisdom. I, too, had grown in wisdom and experienced personal healing as well.

When I think back on the whole experience now, I realize what a privilege it is to be a teacher. For in teaching others, I often learn something myself. Yet in this case even more was accomplished. For abortion is not just an academic subject but rather a wound which needs the healing touch of Christ. And only to the extent that we allow Christ to heal our own pain over abortion will we be able to go forth, gently speaking the truth in love, bringing Christ's healing to others.

# WILL ABORTION MAKE ME HAPPY?

## CHAPTER TWO

## ABORTION HISTORY, FACTS, AND FIGURES

The term "Abortion" comes from the Latin "aborir" which means "to perish." It may be defined in a modern sense as the intentional loss of an embryo/fetus within the generative organs of the mother. In particular after implantation in the uterus and before the embryo/fetus is developed enough to live outside the womb. The term is also applied, though less properly, to cases in which the unborn child becomes viable (able to survive outside the womb) yet fails to survive patrician from the mother.

The word "miscarriage" is also sometimes applied, in a wide sense, to both conditions with the key distinction being that abortions are intentionally induced while miscarriages are not.

Both chemical and surgical abortions have been going on since the ancient world. Since abortion is of great controversy, mainly with regard to when human life begins, it might be useful to understand how the classical world understood this relationship.

Before the advent of modern biology in the nineteenth century the ideas of Aristotle had a rather long and remarkable influence in this field and, even in our own day, his ideas are still sometimes referenced. Aristotle had conjectured that at conception an embryo was only endowed with the principle of vegetative life (the life of nourishment and growth) and that the principle of a rational soul (a human soul) was only endowed later. Since the impartation of a rational soul would seem to mark the beginning of human life for Aristotle, his ideas suggest that male offspring are not actually human until 40 days after conception and female offspring are not actually human until 80 days after conception. This seems to suggest that aborting a male child before the 40th day is licit and aborting a female child before the 80th day is, also, licit.

Remarkably, even in the twenty-first century, the speaker of the House Nancy Pelosi cited these obviously unscientific and sexist ideas while defending abortion in 2008.

> *I would say that as an ardent, practicing Catholic, this is an issue that I have studied for a long time. And what I know is, over the centuries, the Doctors of the Church have not been able to make that definition … St. Augustine said at*

*three months. We don't know. The point is, is that it shouldn't have an impact on the woman's right to choose"*
*https://www.liveaction.org/news/nancy-pelosi-outrageous-abortion-remarks*

What is even more remarkable here is that Pelosi, a supposed feminist, was referencing a period when female children could licitly be aborted while male children could not!

The early church did much to improve the position of women in the world. In the Roman Empire females were thought to be of less value than males and abortion and infanticide were common. Thus, female babies were often victims of these horrific practices than males. "The Didache" is a first century document used to train new converts to the Christian faith. It is quite explicit about the prohibition of both abortion and infanticide for Christians:

> *You shall not murder a child by abortion*
> *nor kill that which is born"* Didache.
> The Teaching of the Twelve Apostles
> (translation Roberts-Donaldson).

The early Christians were so effective at preventing these cruel practices that, within a brief period of time, there were a greater number of female than male children in the general population.

Many of these women chose to dedicate their lives to God as celibates. Out of practical considerations they soon began to gather into communities of Christian nuns. As Owen Chadwick points out in his book: A History of Christianity this was another positive step forward for women:

> *…as women gathered into communities,*
> *some of them learned to read and write,*
> *for a community needed members who*

*could read the bible to them and could talk about it"* (Chadwick, 0., (1995). A history of Christianity p. 77. New York: St. Martin's press).

In these early communities of nuns, women could often come and go as they pleased and even choose to leave the community all together in order to marry. They were a great step forward for women in general and places of safely, stability, and education.

The topic of women's rights and abortion is both a very important and very misunderstood one. For, historically speaking, females have been the targets of abortion much more than males. In both the East and the West for various reasons male children have long been preferred. One can look to the ancestor worship of China, the first-born son receiving the blessing of the father in Judaism, and even the need for male heirs in feudal Europe and understand why females have long been more a target of both abortion and infanticide than males.

At the turn of the twentieth century the eugenics movement arose. "Eugenics" is a composite of two Greek words which mean "well born." The term was actually coined in 1883 by Francis Galton who was a cousin of Charles Darwin. This was appropriate enough as eugenics was based upon a rather simplistic view of heredity theory combined with a lethal mixture of social Darwinism. The general idea was that certain human beings are born with observable traits which make them incapable of being successful in society. Not surprisingly, the traits which were considered "normal" were those of the ruling white Anglo Saxon protestants (WASPs) and the traits which were considered "abnormal" were those of other mostly southern or eastern European immigrants and other ethnic minorities altogether.

At its peak in the nineteen twenties eugenics was not a fringe but quite a mainstream movement in the United States. It was packaged as the "quest for healthy babies" and led to many famous cases of the forced sterilization of those persons, or groups of persons, considered to be "abnormal."

According to PBS, the eventual founder of Planned Parenthood, Margaret Sanger, was quite active in the eugenics movement. (https://www.pbs.org/wgbh/america nexperience/features/pill-eugenics-and-birth-control/).

Sanger's main cause was birth control in general, yet she hitched her wagon up willingly to the eugenics movement. In a 1919 edition of "Birth Control Review" in an article entitled "Birth Control and Racial Betterment" Sanger wrote the following:

*Eugenics without birth control seems to be a house built upon the sands. It is at the mercy of the rising stream of the unfit*

Further, in a letter to Doctor Clarence Gamble in 1939 Sanger wrote the following:

*We don't want the word to go out that we want to exterminate the negro population.*

Such statements by the founder of the number one abortion provider in the United States, ironically named "Planned Parenthood," seem to suggest that abortion is less about women's rights and more about the eugenics movement.

This same eugenics movement inspired Adolf Hitler's views on racial purity which eventually led to the Holocaust. And this connection between the eugenics movement and abortion goes on to our very own day.

A recent CBS news report on how Iceland is (supposedly) eradicating down syndrome revealed that what was really going on is that all fetus' suspected of having the condition were being systematically aborted: https://www.cbsnews.com/news/down-syndrome-iceland/ . Although this report is hardly representative of Iceland's treatment of people with special needs in general, its does point out the continuing relationship between abortion and eugenics.

Alveda King, who is the niece of Doctor Martin Luther King Jr., holds that the relationship between abortion and eugenics continues today and that Blacks are particularly targeted: Alveda King on Disproportionate Abortion of Black Babies: 'That's Certainly Black Genocide' | MRCTV Yet do the numbers bear this out?

The CDC publishes an "Abortion Surveillance" report annually. The latest version of this report states the following:

> *White women had the lowest abortion rate (5.7 abortions per 1,000 women aged 15–44 years) and ratio (106 abortions per 1,000 live births), and Black women had the highest abortion rate (24.4 abortions per 1,000 women aged 15–44 years) and ratio (429 abortions per 1,000 live births).*
> *Abortion Surveillance — United States, 2022 | MMWR*

In the United States 24.4/1000 Black children are aborted compared to 11.6/1000 Hispanic children and 5.7/1000 White children. Thus, Black children are aborted at almost five times the rate of White children and Hispanic children are aborted at about twice the rate of White children! Doctor Alveda King is very clear and unambiguous in her analysis of this:

> The numbers are higher in the African American community, so that's certainly black genocide," she said. "But abortion is genocidal in nature, and it is a eugenicist plot.

Therefore, we see in the history of abortion that it has hardly been a wonderful practice that has lifted up the rights of women but, rather, a horrific practice which has been systematically used to destroy unwanted persons or groups be they female, people with special needs, or ethnic minorities.

# Pregnancy Facts

-The development of life begins with conception.

- Sperm penetrates the ovum which then becomes a zygote.

- A zygote contains all the genetic material needed for a unique human being.

- The zygote migrates to the uterus and expands to become a blastocyst.

- By day ten the blastocyst implants on the wall of the uterus.

- From implantation to the eighth week the term for new life is "embryo."

- In this phase the major organs form, and the heart begins to beat yet the embryo is only about 1" long.

- In week seven the facial features form, major muscles develop, and the heart beats twice as fast as its mother.

- In week eight every organ is present, brain waves can be measured, and hands are sensitive to touch.
- In week nine the technical term for new life is now "fetus" ("offspring").
- The hands now bend at the wrist, fingernails are present, nerves are functioning, and sex organs appear.
- In week ten facial expressions occur, teeth are forming, and spontaneous movement occurs.
- With everything present all that really needs to happen now for the about 2 1/2" long fetus is to grow.
- Although movement is already present, around weeks 16-20 the mother feels the "quickening."
- In week 22-24 the ability of the fetus to live outside the womb with medical intervention occurs.
- In week thirty ninety-eight per cent of babies born will survive.

# Methods of Abortion

- 1-10 days: birth control pills prevent implantation.
- 1-9 weeks: "abortion pills" like RU486 provoke contractions of uterus to expel fetus.
- 1-3 weeks: an abortionist expands uterus and uses syringe to remove embryo.
- 4-12 weeks: the abortionist widens cervix and inserts thin flexible tube into uterus. A strong vacuum device then provides suction which rips the embryo apart and suck it out of uterus.
- 12 weeks: the abortionist widens cervix and then uses combination of forceps and strong vacuum suction to pull pieces of fetus out of uterus.
- Late term abortion (really any time before baby is born):
- Saline injection: the abortionist injects saline (salt) solution into the

amniotic fluid, which surrounds fetus, in order to induce labor contractions. This solution burns the quite sensitive skin of the fetus before inducing birth. Some babies survive this method yet are left to die from exposure.

- Partial birth abortion: the abortionist induces labor and then cuts the spinal cord before the baby is fully delivered. The abortionist Kermit Gosnell was convicted of mass murder in 2014 after repeatedly using this method. Https://www.operationrescue.org/archives/gosnell-post-script-how-they-were-sentenced/links to an external site.

- Other methods may be cited as many have been developed to get around the letter of the law in places which forbid late-term abortion.

# *Abortion Facts and Figures

- There are about one million abortions per year in the United States.
- The abortion rate has been declining since 1990.
- There have been about sixty million abortions in the United States since 1973.
- Most western nations have lower abortion rates than the United States.
- 1.5 percent of abortions per year are due to rape or incest (although this could be under reported).
- The CDC reports that three women a year die from abortion (although this is likely under reported).
- The CDC reported abortions by age in 2021 as being: 15 & under: .2%, 15-19: 8.1%, 20-29: 57%, 30-39: 31.2%, 40 and over: 3.6%.
- Estimated abortions by minors (under 18) 7-8%.

- The CDC reported the following abortion by ethnicity rates for 2022: Black: 24.4/1000, Hispanic 11.6/1000, White 5.7/1000.
- Notice that Blacks have an abortion rate almost 5 times higher than Whites and that Hispanics have an abortion rate twice as high as Whites. This has led some to call abortion a form of ethnic genocide.

*Taken from both CDC and Guttmacher Institute statistics as found on Facts About Abortion: U.S. Abortion Statistics

# WILL ABORTION MAKE ME HAPPY?

# CHAPTER THREE

# The Abortion Arguments

There are broad, implied, and specific arguments in favor of abortion. Let us begin with a broad one. It is often implied that abortion is a right. Phrases like "My right to an abortion" or "Women's reproductive rights" are often heard. Therefore, the question should be asked, "Can abortion be thought of as a right?"

The term "right" may have several meanings yet the strongest of them refers to the tradition of human rights. However, when one makes the claim that something is a human right, they are making a claim that goes beyond law or tradition to something quite basic. The founder of human rights Francisco Suarez based the concept not just on divine law, for he was a Jesuit, but also in the notion of just relationships between persons.

In the context of abortion, the main relationship referred to is between the mother and the unborn child. So just what did Suarez say about just relationships and rights? He said that within just relationships between persons there are certain things so basic that one should not only talk of them existing between persons, but within each person. Therefore, the question must be asked whether a just relationship between persons can exist where one person takes the life, or hire an agent to take the life, of another?

Clearly the answer here, with extremely limited exceptions, is no. One can speak of the right of self-defense and point out that a situation could exist where one person was directly threatening the life of another, and the person threatened had to use deadly force in defending themselves. This argument of a right of self-defense is often used in pro second amendment circles to ground the right to bear arms. Yet does an unborn child ever threaten the life of a mother in such a willful way? Absolutely not!

Now one could continue the argument for a right to abortion by saying that it is grounded in another right. This is often done in terms of the right to privacy and, in fact, is the argument that the infamous Roe v. Wade Supreme Court ruling was based upon. The problem here is that the principle of the fundamentality of rights states that my rights end where another person's rights begin, and that the right to life is clearly a more fundamental one than the right to privacy. Therefore, we begin to see that any language which implies a right to an abortion is, in reality, pseudo language not based in fact or tradition but only rhetoric.

An implied argument for abortion which one often hears is the familiar pro-abortion saying "I can do whatever I want with my own body." The reason I call it implied is that when attempting to put this argument into syllogistic form there is an obvious unstated yet implied premise:

*Major premise: I can do whatever I want with my own body.*
*Minor (implied) premise: The fetus is a part of my body.*
*Conclusion: Therefore, I can get an abortion if I so choose.*

While the logic is valid in this syllogism both the major and the minor premises are problematic. The premise, "I can do whatever I want with my own body", is I believe spoken by most abortion supporters with regard to the right of privacy. However, the problem here is that this is clearly a moral, and a privacy, argument. So much so that the very description of the "Moral Issues" course we are now taking at San Jose State University states that abortion is the first issue we should talk about.

Further, the minor premise "the fetus is a part of my body" is clearly by any modern scientific measure false. Perhaps back in the 1970s before there was good imaging technology and genetic science one could get away with such statements.  However, we now clearly know that even as an embryo the developing human being has its own circulatory system and brain waves and ability to feel pain. Yet, beyond that, we now clearly know through genetic science that it has its own DNA code. Therefore, this syllogism is unsound in that both the major and minor premises are false.

Our course textbook "Doing Ethics" has many arguments in favor of abortion. Judith Jarvis's Thompson's essay "A Defense of Abortion" is interesting because she starts out by conceding the point that a fetus is a human person. This is quite an important concession because in Roe v. Wade the Supreme Court made the distinction between "human being" and "human person" rather critical to their decision. Therefore, in effect, Thompson begins her essay by admitting that the Roe v. Wade decision was wrong!

After conceding the status of human person to the fetus Thompson then uses her famous "violinist analogy" to argue for her point. The analogy basically states that being pregnant is like waking up one day chained in bed to a violinist who is surgically hooked up to your kidneys (talk about the need for dialysis reform!). And then having to stay chained to that violinist in bed for nine months (the human gestation period).

Two things are really at play here: the quality of the analogy and the nature of consent. Therefore, we must ask two questions: "Is being chained in bed to a violinist for nine months analogist to being pregnant?" And "What is the nature of consent here?"

It seems to me that the first question is easily answered by simply observing any woman who is having a normal pregnancy. For women in this state are hardly bedridden but usually quite active particularly in the early part of pregnancy and often even into the late. My own mother told the story of her pregnancy with me and said that my birth was basically induced by her working hard in the garden tending to her roses on a hot summer day. So, although there are extremely limited exceptions, the vast majority of pregnancies are not at all like Thompson's violinist analogy.

The second part of the argument is a familiar one in many of the "Me Too" conversations of our day. Mainly, did the woman consent? And since Thompson's violinist's analogy clearly involves a situation where the woman did not consent it follows that her argument may only be applied to similar situations. Obviously, this involves pregnancies causes by rape or incest. We know from our careful description of the facts that these are about 1.5% pregnancies and are most likely underreported. Therefore,

Thompson admits here that her argument applies to only 1.5% of pregnancies and this, of course, assumes that her argument by violinist analogy is a good one (which it is in fact not). Yet let us concede this point for now.

The "Bell Curve" or Standard Normal Distribution represents how data is normally clustered in nature. For example, most people are around average height while some are quite short and some quite tall. Therefore, if you take the middle of the curve and add up 15% + 19.1% + 19.1% + 13% you see that 68.2% of people (the entire middle part of the curve) are around average height while only 15.9% of people are quite short or quite tall. When you move far out to the left tail of the curve you see how few pregnancies Thompson's argument really applies to. For even being generous and saying rape and incest are responsible for 1.7% of pregnancies (and not the reported 1.5%) one sees that this is only the small tail of the distribution left of the 1.7% dividing line.

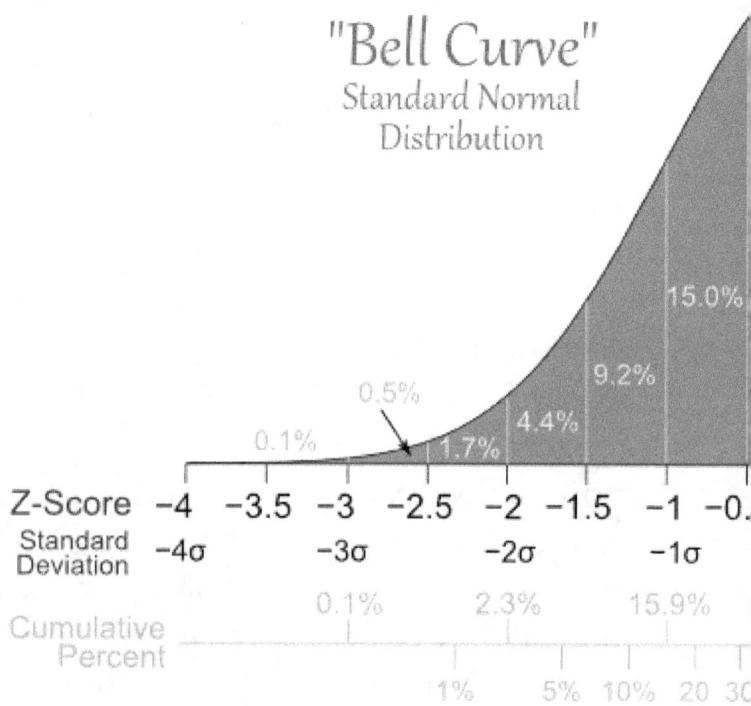

Let us be clear at this point that this is in no way to discount the moral depravity of rape and incest or the suffering it brings to its victims but, rather, to simply add clarity to our discussion.

Perhaps realizing this, Thompson then at the very end of her essay attempts to add pregnancies due to "defective contraception" to the logical category of pregnancies which do not involve consent. Not only is this an affront to the victims of rape and incest but it is also logically quite problematic.

The question now becomes, "When I use contraception am I consenting to the possibility of pregnancy?" While modern so called "health" experts might lead you to believe not, the fact is that even the most effective forms of contraception have high rates of failure. For example, take condoms. Condoms are passed out like candy canes on many university campuses and are hailed as being highly effective against both pregnancy and STD infection yet just how effective are they really?

The largest abortion provider in the United States admits that in real world use condoms are only 85% effective. (https://www.plannedparenthood.org /learn/birth-control/condom/how-effective-are-condoms). This means that using a condom is a lot like playing Russian roulette. For one divided by six gives you a 16.7% chance that a six-shot revolver will go off and condoms fail 15% of the time. Yet then, what is the chance that the revolver will go off if one pulls the trigger six times instead of one?

Therefore, one sees that the very notion of perfectly effective birth control that always prevents pregnancy is a fantasy and not a fact. Meaning that, Thompson's assertion here is simply not in line with the facts.

Can her argument perhaps be saved though?  Not in terms of her false "defective contraception" assertion but in terms of some other situations which might exist in which consent is not really given to the sex act itself (and therefore not to the pregnancy). I would argue "Yes." However, this will hinge upon if one wants to consider statutory rape as being analogist with rape and incest? Now in statutory rape a minor is said to have not given consent not because they did not agree to the sex act itself, but because they are not capable of agreeing to a sex act in general. The CDC reports that 8.3% of abortions are done on women under 18 years of age. Assuming, of course, that about ¾ women who recently turned 18 got pregnant while still 17 we can take a little off this statistic and say that about 8% of all abortions are done on women who conceived as minors. Yet even in doing this and adding the 1.7% of rape and incest victims (many of whom are most likely minors as well) we see that Thompson's argument only applies to around 9% of all abortions. Therefore, in effect, even being generous to Thompson's argument we see it only effects a rather small number of abortions. However, I think quite importantly, we have now created a principle where one can say abortion is licit if consent was not involved in the pregnancy.

Taking this principle even further, we could say that in this new system every time a woman gets an abortion she did not consent to the pregnancy. Therefore, in all cases an investigation should be conducted. This would help us root out of society those predatory males who commit rape, incest, and statutory rape and thus make our world a better and safer place for women and young girls to live in.

Let us now move on to Mary Anne Warren's "On the Moral and Legal Status of Abortion" essay. One of the most interesting aspects of this pro-abortion article are the many pro-life arguments contained within it. She begins by refuting Jarvis Thompson's body as property argument:

> *Furthermore, it is probably inappropriate to describe a woman's body as her property since it seems natural to hold that a person is something distinct from their property (<u>Doing Ethics</u> p. 185).*

Then, speaking of Jarvis Thomson's "violinist" argument she states:
> *Her argument is based upon a clever, but I think faulty, analogy. She asks us to*

*picture ourselves waking up one day, in bed with a famous violinist... This argument is initially quite plausible, and in the extreme case of pregnancy due to rape is probably conclusive... But what are we to say about the woman who becomes pregnant not through rape but because of her own carelessness, or because of contraceptive failure... The crucial difference between a pregnancy due to rape and the normal case of an unwanted pregnancy is that, in the normal case, we cannot claim that a woman is in no way responsibly for her predicament (<u>Doing Ethics</u> p. 186-187).*

This is all quite logical, yet when Warren turns to her own positive argument of "Moral Community" it hardly seems any more plausible than the Judith Jarvis Thompson argument she has just so well refuted.

In her argument, Warren essentially sets up a criterion of observed behavior which makes a thing "human" and thus eligible to be a part of the human "Moral Community."

> *I suggest that the traits which are most central to the concept of personhood, or humanity in the moral sense, are, very roughly, the following:*
> *1. Consciousness (of objects and events external and/or internal to the being), and in particular the capacity to feel pain.*
> *2. Reasoning (the developed capacity to solve new and relatively new and complex problems).*
> *3. Self-motivated activity (activity which is relatively independent of genetic or direct external control).*
> *4. The capacity to communicate, by whatever means, messages of an indefinite variety of types.*
> *5. The presence of self-concepts, and self-awareness, either individual or communal, or both."*

The problem with Warren's "Moral Community" criteria is that, while traits 1, 3, and 4 in reality argue against abortion, traits 2 and 5 make not only abortion licit but, in fact, infanticide as well! With regard to arguing against abortion, we know through fetal science that a fetus has the ability to feel pain at 20 weeks (trait 1). And in the "quickening", also at 20 weeks, to engage in self-motivated activity and to on some level communicate (traits 3 & 4). With regard to arguing for infanticide, we know through child development theory that reasoning (trait 4) as Warren describes it does not happen until around age 7, and self-awareness (trait 5) until around age 2. Therefore, Warren's "Moral Community" criteria seem to be arguing both against abortion and for infanticide at the same time! Thus, it is fitting to say that Mary Anne Warren's "Moral Community" argument is not only false, but dangerously incoherent as well.

# WILL ABORTION MAKE ME HAPPY?

# CHAPTER FOUR

## LETTERS TO THE EDITOR

While a student at San Jose State University I received several opportunities to publicly speak out about the life issue in classroom conversations and in the pages of our university newspaper "The Spartan Daily." The following letters are responses to original letters or columns not present here. However, I think they stand well alone, and I am proud to say that the letter "Abortion and the Holocaust Have Real Similarities" was actually used for many years by an English professor as an example of a good analogy.

# ALUMNUS CRITICIZES EDITOR

The Spartan Daily dropped to a new low in Terri K. Milner's "Catholic Church out of Touch" column! When did it become acceptable at the Daily to ridicule students for their religious beliefs because they criticize the obvious poor taste of your paper? Would you have responded in such a low-handed manner if the faith in question was Islam or Judaism? I think not. Thus, the anti-Catholic bias of the Spartan Daily has once again been confirmed.

It is well known that condoms have only an 80 to 90 percent success rate (if a person actually remembers to wear them in the first place). Yet your paper continues to spread the myth about so-called "safe sex" with a condom.

Well, I have news for the Spartan Daily—rubber does break! Thus, in fact the only "safe sex" is no sex at all or in a monogamous relationship with a person who has not been infected with a sexually transmitted disease to begin with. How might one do this? How about proudly remaining a virgin until you are married? And this is what the Catholic Church chooses to teach its members.

In a society where 72 percent of high school seniors have had sex, the moral teachings of the Catholic Church stand as a beacon of light on a dark sea. Young people realize deep in their hearts that they want to be loved for who they are, and not just for the pleasure their bodies can bring. Yet your paper continues to peddle the failed ideas of "sexual freedom." And what is this "sexual freedom" a freedom to? Unwanted pregnancy? Sexually transmitted diseases? A teenage suicide rates run out of control?

Yet the most offensive suggest of all made in Milner's column was suggesting the Catholic Church is engaging in modern-day genocide by teaching that condoms are a formula for disaster. If we wish to discuss genocide, let us talk about the million babies a year murdered in their mother's wombs as a result of the "sexual freedom" you are so quick to peddle. Where is their freedom?

This now brings us full circle to the reason for the anti-Catholic bias which exists at the Spartan Daily.

I offer this for consideration. What voice stands in society consistently calling for responsible sexual behavior and respect for human life? The voice of the Catholic Church stands as the lone "voice crying in the wilderness" (Mark 1:31). It is a voice which speaks of truth, life, and the love that God has for every human person. Many wish to silence this voice through bias and ridicule, yet I have news for them — truth can never be silenced, yet it can always set you free!

John C. Wilhelmsson

Alumnus

# WILL ABORTION MAKE ME HAPPY?

# BIRTH CONTROL PILLS ARE NOT CURE ALLS

Stepanie Entwistle complains that the Spartan Daily "left out some very important facts about birth control pills" and then goes on to present one of the most distorted pro-pill diatribes I have ever read while totally ignoring all of the dangerous truths about the pill.

The birth control pill is one possible treatment for certain women with genuinely pathological conditions like such as serious hemorrhaging. Yet to suggest that a treatment good in a few particular cases should be used in all cases is absurd. After all, electric shock therapy has been proven effective in certain serious cases of depression, yet I doubt any one of us would wish to be hooked up to the electrodes just because we are feeling a bit down?

Yet the far greater problem her letter is that the birth control pill has in fact been shown to have many damaging physical side effects, such as circulatory problems, a greater risk of ectopic pregnancy, and a higher presence of malignances of the genital tract which are associated with cancer.

Further, in many cases, birth control pills do not prevent conception but rather prevent the implantation of the fertilized egg on the uterus wall thus actually causing very early term abortion which not only destroys the possibility of life but also opens up the mother to further harmful physical and psychological side effects such as a greater risk of breast cancer.

The good news is that safe and natural methods are available. Call the Couple to Couple League at (800) 745-8252.

John C. Wilhelmsson

Graduate Student

Philosophy

# ABORTION AND THE HOLOCAUST HAVE REAL SIMILARITIES

Daniel Offerman's comparison of Abortion to the Holocaust of the Jews by the Nazis in World War II recently drew an unfavorable response from Allison Beltz.

While I believe that the tone of Mr. Offerman's original letter, one of severe indignation, is certainly not helpful to the abortion debate, I am still not as prepared as Ms. Beltz seems to be to throw out the Holocaust/Abortion analogy altogether.

In preparing the way for the Holocaust, the Nazis used a two-part strategy. The first part of this strategy was to say that Jews were not human beings, or at least were not as important of human beings as they were, and the second part of this strategy was to say that the Jews were, in effect, their enemies because the Jews held them back from being all they were destined to be.

Those who promote abortion also use a two-part strategy. The first part of this strategy is to say that unborn children are not human beings, or at least are not as important of human beings as they are, and the second part of this strategy is to say to women that unborn children are, in effect, your enemies because they will hold you back from being all you are destined, or "choose," to be.

In both cases, the "solution" put forth to the problem is that the sub-human enemies to our destiny must die. This "final solution" resulted in the killing of six million Jews in World War II and has, so far, resulted in the killing of 40 million unborn children since abortion was legalized in 1973.

Women are also the victims of abortion. The procedure killed many women before 1973, and women continue to die today as a result of it. Those women who survive face a 30 percent greater risk of breast cancer and the severe depression, known as "Post Abortion Syndrome", both of which bring even more harm.

We live in a nation today that is economically rich, yet morally poor.

Mother Teresa of Calcutta said it best:

> *To me, the nations with legalized abortions are the poorest nations. The great destroyer of peace today is the crime against the innocent unborn child.*

If we truly want peace and justice in our world today, we must stop asserting the "right" of one group over another and start respecting all human beings based on their inalienable rights. And none of these rights is more basic than the right to life.

John C. Wilhelmsson

Graduate student

Philosophy

# WILL ABORTION MAKE ME HAPPY?

# BUSH'S PRO-LIFE POLICY HAS ITS ROOTS IN DECLARATION

I am writing in response to Michelle Jew's rather unfortunate "Spoiled" column from Wednesday.

I was in Washington, D.C. and participating in the "March for Life" along with a half-million other peaceful and prayerful pro-life people. I took part in the cheers as President Bush's statement, getting U.S. tax dollars out of the international abortion business, was read.

President Bush's action came exactly eight years after former president Bill Clinton, just two days into office, reversed a long-standing U.S. policy and funded abortion all over the world with our tax dollars.

President Bush's actions affirming the culture of life exactly mirrored former President Clinton's action which had affirmed the culture of death.

Another thing the Clinton administration "accomplished," as Ms. Jew would say, in regard to abortion, was his twice vetoing of a ban on partial birth abortion (which legalizes killing a newborn child as long as that child has as little as his or her big toe left inside of the mother). I am confident President Bush will soon put an end to this horrific practice as well.

Ms. Jew's definition of a prolife person is flawed both in its premise and its logic. The actual source of the "Right to Life" movement comes not from religion but from the Declaration of Independence, which states:

*We hold these truths to be self-evident, that all men are created equal, that they are endowed by their Creator with certain unalienable rights, that among these are life, liberty and the pursuit of happiness.*

However, it has always been accepted that these rights can be forfeited if a person, by their own choice, commits certain acts of hostility toward society.

The 132 executed criminals in Texas had committed such acts and thus paid the consequences. However, the 40 million unborn children slaughtered by abortion since 1973 had no such choice. For they were all, by definition, innocent. And this includes those who posed a threat to the mother's health or were conceived as a result of rape. For unborn children are, quite simply, innocent in all cases.

The most chilling fact is that if you were born after 1973, approximately one-third of your generation has already been killed by abortion. And the many young people coming to a realization of their own survival of abortion is the reason why the pro-life movement is younger and stronger than ever.

John C. Wilhelmsson

Graduate student

Philosophy

# WILL ABORTION MAKE ME HAPPY?

# WOMEN IN NEED CAN FIND SUPPORT IN CHRISTIANITY

I was rather disappointed by the perverted and false view of Christianity put forth by Jake Huether in his March 1 letter to the editor.

Christianity, by definition, is about being like Jesus Christ, as he is portrayed in the Gospel of John, chapter eight. Christianity is never about condemning. No matter what poor choices a woman has made in her past, Christians are called to bring practical help, forgiveness, and truth to such situations. Huether also wrote, "Christians do not offer genuine financial help to deter abortion." This statement is, quite simply, false. Many

Christian organizations offer practical help to a woman facing a crisis pregnancy. The Juan Diego Society has been doing this in San Jose for the past 15 years. And a woman who is facing a crisis pregnancy need only to call them to receive such help.

As a Catholic Christian, I stand ready, through my support of the Juan Diego Society, to help any woman here at San Jose State University facing a crisis pregnancy. I challenge all Christians on campus to join me in this effort so we may stop throwing stones and start being the hands and feet of Christ.

John C. Wilhelmsson

Graduate student

Philosophy

# WILL ABORTION MAKE ME HAPPY?

# ABORTION ALSO A RESULT OF A VIOLENT SOCIETY

I am writing in response to Dapo Ashaolu's criticism of Christina Lucarotti's column, published May 1. Lucarotti was absolutely correct in linking the brutal rape of a 7-year-old girl, just two miles from campus to our violent just-beneath-the-surface society. How many little girls and boys must be harmed before we admit that our society has a problem, and we begin to search for a cause and solution? Does the long list of tragic names — Kevin Collins, Polly Klaas, Xiana Fairchild, and Jon Benet Ramsey — have to go on forever?

Actually, the only problem with Lucarotti's column was that she did not go far enough and make the obvious link. Forty million children have been violently killed in their mother's womb since abortion on demand was legalized in 1973 and since that same time, the child abuse rate, outside of the womb, has also skyrocketed. America, get a hint! You can't murder 40 million children in their mothers' wombs and expect to have a society safe for children.

Until each child is welcomed as a precious gift, from conception to completion, the slaughter will continue both inside and outside of the womb.

John C. Wilhelmsson

Graduate student

Philosophy

# WILL ABORTION MAKE ME HAPPY?

# ABORTION IS UNSAFE FOR WOMEN AND CHILDREN ALIKE

I am writing in response to Julie Crabill's response to my letter to the editor of May 3, which made the connection between abortion and child abuse.

Ms. Crabill writes that abortion is "safe." Beyond the fact that it is certainly unsafe for the child whose death is its purpose (40 million and counting) abortion is unsafe for women as well.

The abortion procedure still kills women today, and beyond this, women who survive abortion face a 30 percent greater risk of breast cancer and severe depression known as post-abortion syndrome. Both of which cause even more harm and death.

This is not "safe."

The point I made about child abuse and abortion goes far beyond just a random correlation because of the direct analogy between children, both inside and outside of the womb, being violently killed in both cases.

As for Crabill's vicious, personal attack against me, one can only say that it is only when one has lost an argument that one must resort to vicious attacks against the personal character of one's adversary.

Furthermore, it was a woman, Mother Theresa of Calcutta, who was the first person to make the connection between abortion and crimes against children. She said:

> *The greatest destroyer of love and peace is abortion, which is war against the child. The mother doesn't learn to love, but kills to solve her own problems. Any country that accepts abortion is not teaching its people to love, but to use violence to get what they want.*

John C. Wilhelmsson

Graduate student

Philosophy

# *CHAPTER FIVE*

# CHRISTIANITY AND SCIENTIFIC METHODOLOGY

I was happy to be asked by the Theology on Tap team to speak on the topic of Christianity and Scientific Methodology. For the very closely related topic of Faith and Reason is one that not only inspired me to become a philosopher but also that I deal with on a regular basis while teaching my Ethics courses at San Jose State University.

Certainly, I hope we are all aware of Pope John Paul II's great Encyclical published on October 15th, 1998, <u>Fides et Ratio</u> (Faith and Reason). He begins this document with a wonderful and almost poetic passage:

*Faith and reason are like two wings on which the human spirit rises to the contemplation of truth, and God has placed in the human heart a desire to know the truth—in a word, to know himself—so that, by knowing and loving God, men and women may also come to the fullness of truth about themselves.*

Pope John Paul II goes on to state that the trouble in the Church today is not as much a lack of faith as it is a lack of reason. An incredible thing for a pope to say and, in reality, the assertion of a problem that my entire career as a philosophy instructor has been an attempt to correct.

In terms of the problem, or one might even say "crisis", of the sciences in our own day, there is an unfortunate tendency for people of any given age to think that their problems are somehow unique when in fact, as any student of the history of thought can tell you, most problems are not really all that unique and, sometimes, even have been dealt with in recent history in very well documented ways.

In fact, the very idea of linear time is a somewhat novel one historically speaking. For many ancient civilizations rather held to the idea of time as an eternal recurrence. Yet, as Christians we know that time has a beginning and an end and that one of the opportunities this presents to us is the ability to look back on our history and seek insights for today.

However, it might be helpful at first to try and get some perspective on the topic of Christianity and Science. In other words, to ask ourselves why we as Christians are so interested in science?

Aristotle has an interesting take on this topic that might serve us well as a starting point. For in his <u>Nicomachean Ethics</u> Book II, he makes a rather interesting, and I think to many modern persons, surprising statement about the relationship between intellectual and moral virtue.

> *Virtue then is of two kinds, intellectual and moral: now intellectual virtue comes originally, and is increased subsequently, by teaching and therefore needs experience and time, while moral virtue comes through habit.*

In other words, what Aristotle is saying here is that being intelligent does not necessarily make a person moral. That, in fact, the two very mechanisms which make up each faculty are different in nature.

In Aristotle's view of moral virtue, to be a just person one should simply do just acts and to be a temperate person one should simply do temperate acts (Aristotle's "Just do it" motto was borrowed by a shoe company some 2500 years later). And when pressed on exactly what just or temperate acts are Aristotle states:

> *Actions, then, are called just and temperate when they are such as the just or the temperate man would do; but it is not the man who does these that is just and temperate, but the man who also does them as just and temperate men do them. It is well said, then, that it is by doing just acts that the just man is produced, and by doing temperate acts the temperate*

*man; without doing these no one would have even a prospect of becoming good.*

The next question to ask it would seem is "Just who then is this just or temperate man? A question that in Aristotle's day was certainly valid yet when asked by a Christian seems rather absurd. Thus, here we see the etiology of the What Would Jesus Do? (WWJD) movement of the late 20th century. As Christians in Jesus have a sure model of moral virtue.

Therefore, if Christianity is primarily about living a life of moral virtue, we are rather mistaken to be engaging in intellectual or, dare I say, "Scientific" pursuits. Aristotle himself describes the uselessness of such pursuits in the following way.

*But most people do not do these [just or temperate acts], but take refuge in theory and think they are being philosophers and will become good in this way, behaving somewhat like patients who listen attentively to their doctors, but do none of the things they are ordered to do. As the latter will not be made well in body by such a course of treatment, the former will not be made well in soul by such a course of philosophy.*

Further evidence of the veracity of Aristotle's distinction between intellectual and moral virtue can be found in that greatest of all modern truth telling sources—the comic book. For what really is a supervillain but a person who has great intellectual virtue yet extraordinarily little, to no, moral virtue? To make the point about the different nature of intellectual and moral virtue even more strongly, most of these sociopathic villains even seem to hold doctoral degrees!

Therefore, if we are hoping to become scientific in order to become good, I am afraid we are sadly mistaken. And we are also sadly mistaken when we assume a greater morality of those who are intelligent and look to scientists for the answers to what properly are moral and spiritual questions.

So just what is the value of Science to Christianity one might ask? In order to pursue this question further, more perspective is needed.

There is a remarkably interesting document known as <u>The Didache</u> or "The Teaching of the Twelve Apostles." It was discovered in a monastery in Constantinople and then published in 1883. It is a very early Catechism, or instruction on Christian living, which some date to around 50AD. In my book, <u>Tales of the Theotokos</u>, I give some context on early Christian life through looking at the instruction of The Didache.

> *The early Church did much to improve the position of women in the world. In the Roman Empire females were thought to be of less value than males and abortion and infanticide were common. Thus female babies were often victims of these horrific practices. "The Didache" is a first century document used to train new converts to the Christian faith. It is quite explicit about the prohibition of both abortion and infanticide for Christians.*
>
> *"...you shall not murder a child by abortion nor kill that which is born."*

The Didache is thus remarkably interesting to those of us in the pro-life movement because it clearly states that one of the basic tenants of Christian life from the very beginning has been to oppose Abortion.

One of the courses I teach at SJSU is entitled "Moral Issues." In describing this course, the university catalog actually mentions Abortion as one of the primary moral issues to be discussed. Before teaching this course, I had been involved in the pro-life movement as a student and later as a board member at The Juan Diego Society Crisis Pregnancy Centre.

Many of you may not remember, but in the early days of the pro-life movement those in favor of Abortion would often make arguments like: "It is just a blob of tissue really, so it is

OK to have an Abortion." Or that old classic argument for Abortion: "I can do what I want with my own body." Which is in reality a part of a syllogism:

*Major premise:* I can do whatever I want with my own body.

*Minor premise* The fetus is a part of my body.

*Conclusion:* Therefore, I can abort the fetus if I so choose.

Now strange as it might seem, although this syllogism is certainly easily refuted, this was at one time a fairly effective argument in favor of Abortion. However, when I present these arguments to young people today there is rarely anyone who even wishes to defend them.

Why is this so? Certainly, we must always remember that the strong moral voice and teaching of the Catholic Church has played a key role in the pro-life movement since the beginning. However, I do not think that this is particularly why we are winning these arguments now.

Rather, scientific breakthroughs like First-Trimester Ultrasonography are now clearly showing that a gestating human being is definitely not just "a blob of tissue." And the mapping of the human genome has led to an almost ubiquitous cultural presence of DNA evidence in mystery stories and crime dramas. Thus, everyone knows that to be a "part of my body" something needs to share my unique genetic code. And that if something has its own unique human genetic code it is indeed a human being. Thus, Science in general, and these two great scientific breakthroughs in particular, have made the old arguments in favor of Abortion now sound almost silly, when laid out in proper syllogistic form, to the younger generation of today. So perhaps intellectual virtue can be of help to morality after all! For certainly the great scientific minds who have brought us these advances are helping people to better see the truth about Abortion.

Yet let us now move on more properly to the subject of scientific methodology.

The concept of scientific methodology would seem to be a simple one. For in setting out to do any particular task the first choice one must make has to do with method. For example, as a locksmith I find it is much easier to bring my lock picks to a lockout than my fishing pole (and of course my fishing pole to the lake to catch fish rather than my lock picks). Yet recently I was talking to a fairly bright young man about scientific methodology. He told me that such questions were best decided by the scientific method. When I, rather stunned at his assertion, confronted him with the argument that the "scientific method" is really just one method among many that a person might use he seemed rather confused at the concept. However, since he is a very handy young man and knows it is better to bring a hammer to drive nails rather than an iPhone, he eventually seemed to get the point.

However, I fear that his confusion about methodology born out of a hyper enthusiasm for the "scientific method" is perhaps not uncommon. Yet, before we trip on our assumptions, we should define our terms.

When I say "scientific method" I mean the good old fashion 2 x 2 experiment where one forms a hypothesis (or prediction of how one variable will effect another). Puts together a control group and an experimental group and has them both perform some sort of a test (involving how the independent variable effects the dependent variable). And then uses some sort of a reasonable decision criterion to say whether the experiment either confirms or does not confirm the hypothesis.

Notice that the method is "inductive" in that one collects information and draws conclusions from particular observations rather than "deductive" when one uses general principles known to be true in order to better understand the particular. Inductive reasoning is thus in many ways the opposite of deductive reasoning. For inductive reasoning makes broad generalizations from specific observations and thus is never true by certainty but only by probability.

This leads us well to my next point. For the hyper confidence in the "scientific method" of our young man seems to be almost an ethos of our age. And such cultural things as ethos really require some sort of a cultural myth commonly put forth in a popular story. Certainly, a story which fits our bill is that of Sherlock Holmes by Sir Arthur Conan Doyle. Conan Doyle's character first appeared at the beginning of the modern scientific age and continues to be very popular today. Thus, my thesis is that Sherlock Holmes is a character who represents in some way both the perceived good and bad sides of modern science.

The character who actually represents the common man in these stories and is indeed in many cases the storyteller himself is Doctor Watson. Almost invariably in these stories a situation similar to the following occurs: A strange man rushes into 221B Baker Street to deliver a dire message to Holmes and Watson and then suddenly leaves. It thus becomes extremely important to the case at hand to know from where the man came. Yet never fear for Holmes invariably knows that the man came from the Piccadilly Circus because he observed a certain kind of mud on his boots and smell on his coat which he believes to be presence only at the Piccadilly Circus (although both could most certainly in theory be presence elsewhere or a product of two separate locations). And when, amazed at Holmes conclusion, Watson invariably states: "That is marvelous Holmes, how did you do it?" Holmes then of course replies: "Simple Deduction dear Watson." And then explains his method.

But wait a minute here! Was the method Holmes used actually Deduction? Absolutely not! For he observed particular evidence to reach his conclusion, and this is the very mark of Inductive, and not Deductive, reasoning. Does Holmes admit that since he is using Inductive reasoning his findings are not by logical certainty but only by statistical probability? Of course not! And here is the crux of the problem. For by claiming that Induction is Deduction Holmes is at the same time claiming that the conclusions of Inductive Science, the "Scientific Method" we have been speaking of, are true by certainty and not only by probability. What is further of interest is that Watson, who after all is a trained physician that should know the difference between Inductive and Deductive reasoning, unquestionably goes along with Holmes assertion. Thus, the popularity of these stories seems definitely wrapped up in this hyper-confident view, which I hope we can now all see is a false view, of "Science" which many of the current generation hold.

Thus, when one hears a supposed "Climate Scientist" say they are "absolutely certain" about global warming and there is no need to investigate it any further they are essentially saying that Inductive reasoning is true by logical certainty, and not just statistical probability. Such a person not only is incapable of doing Science but is also incapable of engaging in coherent logical thought! For even an introductory student of logic knows the distinction between Inductive and Deductive reasoning.

The great philosopher of Science Karl Popper dealt with similar problems in the early twentieth century. Ideologies like Psychoanalysis and Marxism were claiming status as real sciences. Thus,

Popper was challenged to show just how they were not. The key distinction in Pooper's argument being that "Pseudo-Science" is set up to look for evidence which supports its claims, while real Science is set up to challenge its claims and look for evidence which might prove it false. In other words, Pseudo-Science seeks confirmations while real Science seeks falsifications. And I shall leave it you to decide for yourself which camp our hyper-confident "Climate Scientist" falls into.

Another common mistake made in modern Science, and modern thought in general for that matter, is a confusion between the objective and subjective realms. Now before someone starts yelling "get the liberal university professor who only wants to teach subjectivism out of here," please allow me to clarify the point.

Even in Catholic theology itself the distinction is made between objective and subjective redemption. In my book <u>Tales of the Theotokos: Mary in the Personal, Historical, Scriptural, and Spiritual Realms</u> I delve into this point while discussing the meaning of the term "Coredemptrix."

> *In its proper theological definition redemption actually has two aspects. Objective redemption refers to the acquisition of redemptive grace, while subjective redemption refers to the distribution of that same redemptive grace. So, when I speak of using the term "coredemptrix" in a general sense I am actually speaking of using it only with regard to subjective redemption. For when my mother had me baptized, she did not*

help to acquire redemptive grace, for only the sacrificial offering of Christ at Calvary can be said to have done this, but she did help to distribute some of the grace which Christ had already super-abundantly acquired.

Therefore, in the case of subjective redemption, "coredemptrix" is a term that applies not only to the Blessed Mother but rather to any woman who has helped to distribute redemptive grace. For this reason, the proper question to ask is not whether Mary is a coredemptrix, but rather in what particular sense does the term apply to her above all others?

The answer to this question is found in the definition of objective redemption. For many women can be said to have participated in subjective redemption, in releasing redemptive grace, but only Mary *has a claim to have participated in objective redemption, in the acquisition of redemptive grace, as well (p.95-97).*

So, we see here that there is a distinction to be made between the subjective and the objective realms, and, further, that this is a very important distinction for any practicing Christian to be aware of. For I have news for you all brothers and sisters: You and I are never going to participate in objective redemption! For that work of acquiring redemptive grace has already been completed long ago. Our work today thus properly lies in the distribution of grace or subjective redemption. We as Christians are thus workers in the subjective realm.

Pope John Paul II was exceptionally aware of this and, as one of the architects of Vatican II, actually had a strong voice in many of its reforms. Somewhat lost in the essentially political debates about Vatican II are some important truths of the Christian faith that the Second Vatican Council hoped to elucidate. For, as Rocco Buttiglione has pointed out in his fine book <u>Karol Wojtyla: The thought of the Man Who Became Pope John Paul II</u>:

> *One of the goals of the Council was to unify the cause of truth with the cause of human freedom (p. 128).*

Or, as one might say in a more philosophical sense, to unify objective theological truth with subjective human freedom.

The philosophical basis of John Paul II's concerns here can be traced back to his study of the philosophy of phenomenology under the great Polish philosopher Roman Ingarden. Ingarden was both a great friend of Edith Stein (now Saint Teresa Benedicta of the Cross) and a former student of the celebrated founder of phenomenology Edmund Husserl. In his famous lecture "The Crisis of the European Sciences" Husserl had given a vast history of thought in order to help elucidate the current crisis.

Husserl's philosophy grew out of the idea that Western (or European) culture had lost its distinctive purpose. The crisis is thus that philosophy has departed from its original goal to provide answers to human concerns and thus develop the unique capacity of human reason. Thus, Husserl saw human reason as having collapsed and he made his life's work an attempt to save it. The key to the crisis is the place of the Natural Sciences. Like many others, Husserl was impressed by the success of the Natural Sciences yet at the same time he was critical of their assumptions and methods (indeed the "Scientific Method" we have been speaking of). Husserl held that the Natural Sciences rest upon the fatal prejudice that nature is basically physical. Thus, Natural Science holds that the realm of the Spirit, or of human culture, is causally based upon the physical. Husserl sees this as threatening our ability as human beings to know, value, and judge things. Husserl further sees the Natural Sciences as having rejected even the possibility of a science of the human spirit. Husserl holds that this rejection is naïve and that it explains a great deal of the crisis of modern peoples. Naturalism also leads to the idea that knowledge and truth are strictly objective (because it rejects even the possibility of their being a more human and subjective side of things). This problem started when the study of Natural Science and Cultural Science departed from its original unity in ancient Greece.

Philosophy was once a study of both Natural and Cultural science. We can see in a figure like Thales of Miletus a person who is both interested in Natural Sciences, like Astronomy and Meteorology, yet at the same time is interested in more human and subjective concerns. However, Husserl would say that the full flowering of the study of Cultural Science came with the arrival of Socrates and his direct study of more human concerns like

Justice, Piety, and Ethics. This study continued along with this original unity through the classical age (with perhaps Augustine being the last in this line). Later, Rene Descartes made a valiant effort to revive a more human realm of philosophical inquiry with his "Meditations" yet, ultimately, this failed and with the advent of the modern "Scientific Method" the split between Natural Science and Cultural Science was made complete.

Husserl's "Phenomenological Method" was designed to correct this problem by giving us a method that would be as effective with the Cultural Sciences as the "Scientific Method" has been with the Natural Sciences. Husserl's admonition to "bracket off" the prejudices of Natural Science toward the possibility of a science of the human spirit served to open up many of his students to religious faith. Counted among them of course being Edith Stein. Stein's good friend Roman Ingarden eventually became the philosophy professor of Karol Wojtyla. Wojtyla later became a prominent Phenomenologist himself with his work <u>The Acting Person</u>. Then, just as the Second Vatican Council was approaching, Father Wojtyla was consecrated Bishop Wojtyla and thus was given the opportunity to play a significant role in the Council.

Let us now then return to Rocco Buttiglione's rather incredible assertion about Vatican II. For his is an insider's view from a person who was both a friend of John Paul II and a fellow philosopher. He states:

*One of the goals of the Council was to unify the cause of truth with the cause of human freedom (p. 128).*

This idea of unifying the Objective and Subjective realms is very much a phenomenological one. It also matches up nicely to Rene Descartes "Meditations" which Husserl had spoken of in <u>The Paris Lectures</u>: Husserl said of Descartes and his method:

*No philosopher of the past has affected the sense of phenomenology as decisively as Rene Descartes, France's greatest thinker. Phenomenology must honor him as its genuine patriarch. It must be said explicitly that the study of Descartes Meditations has influenced directly the formation of the developing phenomenology and given it its present form, to such an extent that*

*phenomenology might even be called a
new, twentieth century, Cartesianism.*

Yet what had Descartes done exactly
to earn such praise from Husserl to
the point of being considered the great
patriarch of Phenomenology? In my
book <u>Faith, Reason, and the New
Mass Translation</u> I look into this topic:

> *In the discipline of philosophy, we speak
> of Descartes as being the first "modern"
> philosopher. If one had to give a quick
> description of what Descartes did, as a
> philosophy professor must sometimes do,
> it would be that he turned the discussion
> about philosophy into what was going on
> in the subjective experience of the human
> person, and that he wrote his works not
> in the Latin of the universities but in the
> everyday French of his time.*

Is any of this beginning to sound
familiar to you? What if were to

change the subject and paraphrase by stating?

> *The Council sought to turn the discussion about religion into what was going on in the subjective experience of the individual person of faith and it sought to communicate the message of the Church not in its traditional Latin but in the vernacular language of the people.*

Does any of this sound familiar to you now? Yes! Vatican II was quite Phenomenological in nature, not only it its wish to unify human freedom and divine truth, but even in the very ways it chose to do so.

Thus, when you hear people stating their concerns about the 2011 new English Mass translation, please realize that we are not just putting out sour grapes because we don't get to say the same things at Mass any longer, and that we do in fact have serious concerns. For in failing to subjectively connect with people in the real world as well as the old translation did the new English Mass translation has hindered, and not advanced, the Church's ability to unify human freedom with divine truth.

So now we come full circle in seeing that the crisis of modern Sciences is indeed large and is effecting many areas of life including, possibly, the very workings of religious faith. For both the Natural Sciences and many religious faiths seem to have the notion that the Objective realm is all that matters. Thus, the Subjective realm of human spirit, and dare I say human freedom, is minimized or even ignored.

The good news is that this is hardly a new problem, and many solutions are available to us. On a purely philosophical level there is the Phenomenological method itself. With perhaps Edith Stein's philosophy of empathy being a good place to begin. My book <u>Edith Stein: Her Contributions to Philosophy, Feminism, and The Theology of the Body</u> details Stein's early life and philosophy in a way many people have found helpful. I believe that empathy is a key to good ethics thus Stein's philosophy of empathy is studied in all of my Ethics courses.

On the level of a purely Christian renewal the way forward I think is clear. We must realize that, although a sound knowledge of objective redemption is of course necessary, the actual realm of our Christian spiritual life is the realm of subjective redemption. The sacrifice of Christ has objectively and super-abundantly provided grace. Our work now is to find ways to release that grace in the subjective realm around us.

At the very beginning of his pontificate Pope John Paul II uttered the words "Be not afraid." What can these words mean other than that God is with us! Not far away in some objective realm but right here with us in our own everyday subjective experience. Yet it is only when we know with assurance that God is with us that we might abandon ourselves to His will. This is the moment when human freedom becomes united with divine truth. Husserl's philosophy of phenomenology insists that both the objective and subjective realms must be understood and respected. For by doing so we create a bridge toward the cause of truth and the cause of human freedom finding unity.

We see here also the deeper spiritual side of the abortion issue. The Didache tells us right at the start: *"There are two ways, one of life and one of death."* And then tells us in chapter two: *"...you shall not murder a child by abortion nor kill that which is born."* Therefore, when a pregnant woman, in all her human freedom, chooses life she at the same time chooses truth! And this choice is not just one among many but, rather, the very basic of all choices. The choice to unite one's human freedom with divine truth.

## ABOUT THE AUTHOR

John C. Wilhelmsson is a professor of philosophy at San Jose State University. As a professor, John is known for his thoughtful and independent interpretations and intuitive teaching style. Born and raised in San Jose, John became interested philosophy after reading "Fides et Ratio" by Pope John Paul II. He made Edith Stein the focal point of his research because John Paul II mentioned her in this work. With the support of the fine professor of philosophy Richard Tieszen, John began his research on Edith Stein. John was awarded his master's degree in 2007 and his thesis *"The Philosophical Contributions of Edith Stein"* was named best in his college. John is currently a successful businessman and an instructor at San Jose State University.